Human Acts

Human Acts

Heather Spears

Wolsak and Wynn . Toronto

Poems in this book have appeared in *Arc, Canadian Woman Studies / les
cahiers de la femme, Event, The Malahat Review*, and *Poetry Canada Review*.

Cover drawing by Heather Spears
Typeset in Palatino, printed in Canada by
The Coach House Press, Toronto.

The author gratefully acknowledges the support of the
Canada Council. The publishers gratefully acknowledge
support by the Canada Council and the Ontario Arts Council.

Wolsak and Wynn Publishers Ltd.
Don Mills Post Office Box 316
Don Mills, Ontario, Canada, M3C 2S7

Canadian Cataloguing in Publication Data
Spears, Heather, 1934-
  Human Acts
Poems.
ISBN 0-919897-24-X
I. Title.
PS8537.P42H85 1991   C811'.54   C91-093891-1
PR9199.3.S75H85 1991

CONTENTS

PAYING ATTENTION AT POETRY READINGS

I am always moral
at poetry readings
I pay attention, or I try
I always get lost
I begin to rearrange the hair of the poet
or to trim (or eliminate) his beard
I press his trousers
I am fascinated by his fingers
I love his pleasure and his disarming smile
at a particular phrase
I love the little pieces of paper sticking out of his
books

Some poets are austere
they read impatiently
they frown
they do not ingratiate
they dare you to alter their appearance by one thread
they look at you
suddenly
under this kind of pressure
I am dismayed to find
I have again lost track of what they are saying

It is necessary for the poet
to be present
it is to be hoped
that in an audience of twelve or over
(twelve being a respectable, even apostolic number)
that the poem, having been as it were reborn
foundering among the chairs
will be received here and there
by the large if fallible pale ears of the listeners
cupped for it like hands

AT CHICAGO AIRPORT

Lost luggage
does show up, and meanwhile
how clear it remains, almost more clear
in absence, rubbing along the ramp
among the actual stuff that is being
continuously recognized and reclaimed,
almost there, almost as ordinary.
Later, you can't believe
a man won't open that door
marked *no admittance* that you watch
with the mad patience of exasperation,
a man with your bag. There it is!
but it isn't, or not yet.

In this way a lost child
glimpses out of playgrounds and thresholds, a thought
terrible to contemplate.
These are the real ghosts,
with their known bruises and singularities,
the sagging canvas, the red tag from another trip,
the weight you held, and intend to hold.
They are not like the dead,
who are consigned to death,
however vividly, obstinately remembered.

EARTHQUAKE TIME

1

Is unlike ordinary time, or reminds you
time is not ordinary
looking at the precarious hills
pinkish with smog and menace
or driving on the freeway, its brilliant flourishes,
swift gestures and cadenzas,
or going up in an elevator, a box of rapid prayer,
or staring out at low flat buildings
already disordered and spilled into their yards

the structures are afraid, if you are not,
they are deep in thought, they are considering,
crazed, slow, volatile and unreasonable and human —
with such neighbours in your near future
you are definitely on your own
your certainties contract
into a small hereness, an hour in the afternoon,
an orange on a white plate,
a siren somewhere, voices,
the radio playing music and saying
unimportant, sufferable things.

2

is not even that, the moment itself is suspect,
its hold on the past
is its only solid taste and name
what's here has a brim, and it's trembling,
you're asking for it
every time you walk forward
and *deja vu*, whatever you've been told,
is only the right brain
coming in a split second after the left
here you are in earthquake time
wavering between the hemispheres
you can walk all right
but only because walking is
a way to project yourself forward
by continually falling.

9

NIAGARA FALLS FROM THE AIR

says the pilot in a folksy tone
and I find myself
on the wrong side of the plane
(the left-hand passengers craning down,
                                  self-satisfied)
dark dead Lake Ontario fills my window as we bank
for the run into Toronto

while Niagara falls from the air...

in the clear morning, continuously
drop by drop, atom by atom
cascade of landscape
trees with their long shadows
and root systems extended like skirts,
buildings separated into their fragments,
gables and windows
turning in the light, faceted, winking,
fields spilling their snow,
tiny freeways embellishing the distance
like musical signs: diminuendo,
legato...
and the little people of Niagara falling like tapers
drawing their hair down after them
as candles discipline their flame
in an excess of light

and Niagara falls, falls from the air
behind us, blue, luminous, without termination.
We land. We have landed.
Let us reverently deplane.

ROAD SIGNS or THE COMPULSIVE READER IN THE WILDERNESS

How sexual are the highways of my country
Soft Shoulders, Merge, Yield
and a sign that says *Squeeze left*
under which someone has written *Tit.*
Journey's End declares a motel
though we all know very well
it is not / and to some furred mammal
lowflying, nocturnal
and looking down, each vehicle
is a pulse, an infra red
interior of heat in which we are the most hot
crossing bluish winter where only a fox
lights faint and intermittently
among the trees.
Lift the Latch Lodge
will not prosper, false teeth in a glass
hail scraping the windows
Resort implies the last, ice at its shore
cabins shuttered. *The Livettes*
in downtown Sudbury await
the traveller. *Live Bait* says a sign
on a closed store where a traceless track
leads north.
Pool/Sauna we are pools
our blood
contained as yet, we are pods venturing
(*Venture Inn*) we combust internally
we implode, hooded against
profane spill and collision.

There are also wordless signs, yellow and black,
the elate deer,
the stupid cliff with bits falling off one side
skid marks under a silhouetted car
with the driver's head in a gangster's hat.
I love best
the *Runaway Lanes*,
they end in innocence and blackberry
they tempt
terrible events where "failure"
is not a slow
resignation but violent and certain
trucks yearn towards them
Yield

The eye swings to the signs
Elbow Ridge after the *Shoulder* makes the land human
and somehow arthritic / perhaps
Lift the Latch Lodge could thrive
here, a few local changes,
distance contracted into symmetry —
Resort *to* Runaway Lane
Live Bait and *The Livettes*
sharing the stage
in a sad hotel in downtown Sudbury
this *Journey's End* as good as any other
where the highway peters out among buildings and
graves.

FALLING THROUGH

The river of marathon runners
is crossing Key Bridge, and goes on crossing,
under the bright sky and the aeroplanes.
From the fourteenth floor, it looks like play,
each one, I guess, a bundle of nerves,
an intent, and each one gasping.
Last night on K Street, just before sunset,
I passed a man sitting and caught his eye
the way on a bike you'd steer into a stone.
A stare, a redness. Travelling is like
being a kid half scared and laughing
tossed from hand to hand
or those horrible adult games
where you have to pretend to trust
a circle of strangers.
There are times you fall through —
a redness, a glance —
and there is no difference, or,
you see there is no difference.

GOING INTO THE METRO IN STRANGE CITIES

is like getting sick
you don't know anything about it
but once you've carefully and fearfully found your way
you know all about it and you can't remember
it ever was unfamiliar:
the kinds of little tokens to use, and the turnstiles,
the chunky-chunk of the escalator as you descend,
the weepy walls, or flashy tiles
and the thick inhuman, human smell —
and the sound the train makes coming in —
it all becomes ordinary
and you're smart like everyone else and it's easy.
And as the trains hurtle along
(because metro trains have a monopoly on that verb,
                    they always hurtle)
through the tight, but just not too tight, dark —
you know you'll emerge again
even though what you'll find
might be even stranger, but also
easy and habitable after all
like (eventually) death

SEEN FROM THE PETERBOROUGH BUS

The notice on the back of the truck says
in large red letters *BRINE/SLUDGE ONLY*
makes you wonder
what else would anybody be secretly
tempted to add to the load?
what is prohibited?

BRINE/SLUDGE ONLY

Plutonium waste I guess is worse
but somehow
this humble local truck and its sign
are not addressed to larger issues

BRINE/SLUDGE ONLY

no poem has access then, no dreary book on politics,
BRINE/SLUDGE ONLY

what about one white porcelain teacup
decorated with small leaves and violets?
BRINE/SLUDGE ONLY

what about one pearl the shape of a tear?
BRINE/SLUDGE ONLY

or for that matter one tear
(BRINE/SLUDGE ONLY)
the shape of a tear

NIGHT BUS TO PRINCE GEORGE

Two girls got on at Terrace
children, almost, as they passed
I took in,
in this order, their smell
their matted hair, their wretched
packs and clothes.
They sat behind me, talked
like records running down
of a boy one of them "almost fell for"
and one who "finished the section for me yesterday"
"Oh him — I wouldn't —"
suddenly both were asleep, upright,
silence from then on. And the whole time
this smell, recognized instantly,
not cigarettes
or age or illness, just plain sour
animal human dirt —
follicles, cells, pores, the uninhibited skin's
ordinary youth and health.

And as their voices failed in sleep
I thought of the camp — hours on the slope
mosquitos, coughs, a boy calling,
earth under their short nails
grit in the corners of their brilliant eyes
hair shoved back, narrow napes and wrists
scratched from bites and thorns,
then, pissing in the bush,
perfect teeth tearing off bread, squeak and snap
of a Pepsi can,
and the tent, the hard ground
countdown into exhaustion
asleep with their clothes on.

16

I won't smell this again
perfume of tree planters
it's from away back
it's real
drowsing, I wish
it were not wasted on me, I dream
a young, blind man
in my seat, abandoning
his perfect senses to it all night long
drinking this sweetness in.

MELODI GRAND PRIX
(the European Song Contest, 1988)

Her hair's a mass of tiny black curls
her white face is smooth with
the features of the beautiful —
small nose, long exaggerated eyes —
when she opens her red mouth
to the point of dislocation
her head is peeled back, what a thought,
you can see right inside it,
black membrane stretched tight
over papery bone and the thick
and steadying brain just a back wall
under the bush, the teeth
straining like brackets
and no real floor, the throat
an open hose
down into more, and worse

Stop singing, stop opening
this horrible gape, this planetary gasp
out of which are coming
such terrible cries, around which
lights glare, and costumed men
are stroking and striking electrified metal and wood
in order to increase it, or legalize it
or something
in order to make it seem
what we thought we wanted
before we saw what it was.

HOW WOMEN KILL MEN

We do it apparently because of our hearts
whose chambers, in childbirth, yawn
with effort, the mouths of lions,
stationary and dangerous.
We do not clench those tributaries
in our tribulation, our bodies
widen, we are delta and stretched sky,
out of our continent
pours largesse and the gift of years.

In the long verandah against the geraniums
and the traffic, this row of us, these rows,
wait with our white heads, and smile,
you ate what we ate and are extinct
while our wild blood
gushes familiar and unhindered still
behind our knuckled ribs —
we will,
indeed we will.

THE PISSING VIEWS

Oh my sisters
camping in the mountains
all our lives, what are we missing
what disadvantage, what bad news!
the humus steams,
the dark leaf gleams,
but to stand up and piss!
to gaze out, emptying, over the blue abyss!
We'll never have this,
the pissing views!

THE HUMAN HEAD
*The human head is stranger and more mysterious than
the head of a wolf*   Alberto Giacometti

Boulder, planet, lopsided Io
rolls there, tugged, pocked, the rock
a creamy porridge and the sun a star.
Nothing more horrible or valuable.
Those films from the war —
the Japanese, the kneeling man —
how could he kneel, or let
himself be led out to that place and kneel,
his blindfold eyes staring at the close sand?
It occurs. The Arabs touched
the bound hands deftly with the sword's tip
so that the slighter pain
would jerk the head up for the strike.
Wretched, headed man, better to have your brain
elsewhere, to glare
out of the gut than there,
stalked, vulnerable and turning.

Io rolls in the sand, the head
utters, and as if answering
for a short time
the fountain of his body spouts and falls.

Original ball and bowl, trophy of smoke,
the stake's simple dangle and bloom,
the sawdust thud, the drenched
basket, good wood and wood yard
awful with purpose. Piteous brave Charles,
the last laugh,
history's trash and blasphemy.

My students pass the skull from hand to hand.
"Even by touch you know it perfectly,
the human head."
Dearest riddle and dream,
our posy balanced in the graceful wind,
our ache,
our arms its cradle as we sleep,
sometimes across a table
among tired papers, with the light on.

And the heads of others: the child's
in your lap, your mild strokes
intimate and ordinary
Once, empowered hands
pulled or allowed this, foundering, to be born.
Then there is the long night
when you blind yourself in bliss to learn
everything over again
in the rapt reciprocate
grooming of love.
And helpless comfort at its worst —
when what you hold is dangerous —
a swarm, humming with grief and menace.

The clean skull makes its rounds,
and the model enters and calmly sits down;
above her shoulders, over
all her rosy symmetries,
accurate answer
blurred by what we ask,
her human head,
not this brief mask
that faces us, smiling to deceive,
but a rock in darkness bounding who knows where,
a swimmer bobbing on the glassy lake
and grown more distant as we watch.

THE DEATH OF JOHN KEATS

It can go so badly at times.
The entubed child
his Italy one incubator wide
his twin
(familiar strokes, jabs that might have saved him)
kept in a separate box
denied by rituals about
sepsis, contamination —
and love as far as England, countries
of corridors, weight of grief
no balance to correct procedures —
bright light meant for a cure
tiny heel cupped for the modern
letting of blood.

On first looking into
what occurred I almost see
how innocence conspired
against him,
the facts too violent,
the illness graceless to a degree
he couldn't argue —
but he was not blameless, he knew what he was.
Matchless maker, this was very wrong
to let his body burn his mind
out like a torched bowl
and shut his angel's voice
because of blind advice
the worst of deaths,
eye's raisin
fierce neuron
clouding with chosen silence
feeble hand raised
nameless against the untranslated glass
Rome's sickroom puke, and that inadequate friend
a dull, bored nerd
writing and drawing and being kind.

TELLING APART

I am brought to the crib.
There is a brilliance in her eyes
that do not fix and are
all I can comfortably fix on.
The rest, to count what's couth and corrigible
occurred too previously
in failing to occur.
The paired immaculate cells
perfected grain by grain, did not quite meet,
two vehicles in that void place
bypassed their rendezvous.

Nothing is fatal. They can mend
the throat's closure, the fibulae's
false rivulets into the lungs,
make her meek fruits
almost intact.
And now as I draw, by luck
she fists her arms and hands
and hides the black gape under her look.

She has nice hair.
I draw her lash by lash while she stares
randomly at us, with random pleasure.
She will never taste thirst,
or salt. They have told me this.
And something else is missing —
telling apart. She can't get
the trick of it.
There at the fault
a path stops at the brim,
something human never happened.

And as I work I feel
heavy at my brain's root, open wide,
God's leaded book,
long before words, the innate vocabulary
the valuable part that seals
knowing and knowing.
Her mother leans among us at the bars,
graced also by that flicking glance,
not recognized.
As I am razed, graced
by that child's burst face, mine now and theirs
forever and, as I put my pencils down,
all their compassionate, familiar faces.

FOR AN AUTISTIC CHILD

The trouble being that
in spite of my bewitchment
there's nothing to say.
Like having to be near the beloved
which still may seem the stuff of poetry
but is not. People do books now,
TV series called
"the children with the emerald eyes"
— what can I add to that?
Even the clear details
through which you'd come alive
on the page, your toes
fastening on mine under the table
your dilated stare
emerald or whatever
riveted on the blank sky
your hand on the cup, two fingers
dandling in the milk, and all your
other water comforts / here I go
adding my clutter to the media pile
even the one (the toes) through which
I subtly show
(how I hate this in books)
how I "reached" you when I drew,
how you vouchsafed.

You let me, you would not look
at the pictures, maybe once by stealth
you will, if they are left.
So I'm right in line
with the rest, their insights and options
caring and therapies
the lovely longhaired mother rocking for days
to her baby's awful tune, while
her husband films her closeup loveliness.
Or the claims
of the older mother to her son's wild worth
protesting, as she must, as he lumbers
to the swings, his face a fist.

Nobody learns from this,
it is repetitive and bland
Lindsay racing down the river bank
or extending her hand
towards the kettle (and she'll do it)
the brilliance / of her timing
her intelligence
all used and useless except to her intent.
I'm the same, I want to be
cleverest, to prove
something they didn't think of, say it first.

For example that my eye
when I draw you has your look
that can't discriminate, the act
moral only by dint of absolute
moral abdication — the air
pressed to your deliberate turned
cheek, your collar as it intercepts
your nape under your hair
the cup at your wrist's rim —
these have to be as loved and rare
as they think emerald eyes and lashes are.
That's ignorance, at least I know
I am as cruel in my craft
as you appear to be
in your career of ruthless exclusivity.

I can't, I see, stop trying
caught like all the rest
in the net of your condescension;
one flash, and we'll forgive
days, months of our consigned
nonentity, one flash
(your toes) and we'll write tomes
fill up cassettes
the sudden human light
warming the emerald
as you look away —

(It takes so much, Lindsay,
to keep us off,
it takes all you have)

You did not choose us above water, above
the physical unknowable world
and that's our jealousy,
mere maid if I've seen
a fraction of what claims you constantly
I'll have the heart to let you be,
and let you be.

HOW ANIMALS SEE

This is terrible.
It says here
bees can't see yellow.
So the broom, the rape, even the dusty
stamen of the rose
are lurid puce, a shuddery ultra pink,
studied to perfection
over hot millennia how best
to please their lust,
these bits
zooming in for the take
faceted fuzzy cells
the dancing optics of a vast
seduced intelligence.
And as for us
what the flower intends
is less than casual —
utter indifference.
Oh my notched, loved world, atlas of lies,
no longer fit to believe!
and not even mine, not private —
photographed, reassured —
Van Gogh in Arles —
impassioned cadmiums!
Armfuls of buttercups
plundered in childhood
on the Musqueam flats!
And now this maple, frost of gold!
The bees are gone to hive,
in secret, they keep the real real,
their tiny manifold eye
closing in on
the actual valuable
planet, terrible in neon and violet.

Little pieces of the uterine wall
are meandering all over the body
I am guilty of at least five
mutually exclusive illnesses
all situated down below
none studied
in *Health* at Lord Byng High
where year by year we coloured in
the Digestive Tract from esophagus to, well, anus
and the Other, called by my aunts
Curse in a firm rejection of euphemism
was the subject of just one animated film
its pastel voice, embarrassingly, male.
And even now on graphic TV
fluids absorbed by delicate pads are blue
not red, as they are blue
(more understandably) in diaper ads
recalling *potteblå*, a dye
made from kids' piss in the old days.

Little pieces of the uterine wall, it seems
wander and fix in bladder, belly, lung
bleeding there every month, on cue,
crazed little hormones simmering.
Fistulae like tiny fingers
feel out of one organ, fasten in another,
ominous pressures build, great fibrous balls
like twine grow eyeless in the dark
"as large as a twenty-week fetus"
the whole lot hangs
in a drooping hammock of tired flesh
the plug's loose / prolapse
threatens like a sock turned inside out
I may be unable
to contain myself
much longer, I will become
this aspect, with a mind of its own, even
facial expressions, yawns,
grins, and other mouthy blatherings.

Meanwhile the ovaries
plugged in at each side like earphones,
pick up the distant tick of death.

Oh my body, how awful,
you bore children faultlessly
and from these territories
loved, love and are made happy.
How can I read
this book in which everything possible goes wrong
nothing stays where it ought
inside the tidy lines of diagrams,
bits of the uterine wall
slither away, and a cell
I never heard of casually ignites?

WELLNESS OF THE ESOPHAGUS

Again, some horrible new
illness heard of, suffered by
someone almost unknown
or read about in articles
Penile Carcinoma (not me that time)
Cancer of the Esophagus
and the area concerned
pulls in its cells
fastidiously, fear enters
the little distant cupboards of the body

Once Benjamin, aged nine, white faced
when I came to say goodnight —
What's wrong?
but I had to guess, and he asked
how I knew he thought he was dying —
and told me — it was "Heart Cancer".
And I laughed, There's no such thing,
and lied: Kids don't get cancer
anyway (those were the days
in the village, with no TV, no useful,
interesting stuff to scare
the daylights out of them)

I'm wise to it now,
though, and the tellers, when I hear
— crossing the Oak Street Bridge, this time,
and me wedged in the back seat
coming from a funeral —
I won't let
my poor cells cringe
I'll say, almost aloud and breezy:
"I have Wellness of the Esophagus"
and Wellness of who knows
what else, I'll feel good,
oh yes while I can

BULIMIA

is not a nice word
one thinks of
bulbous dimpled arms and bums,
bulk, bulges and bullocks
Bulimia
the medical profession,
men, probably,
could have chosen more courteously
there are lovely words
Islands of Langerhans
where the sky meets the sea
even Leukaemia
lesser goddess, gentle
and Pyorrhoea
although there is something
about little fish in it

Bulimia
I'd rather think of Blake
who ate a whole bottle of linseed oil
one evening
simply because it was there
"Work in the morning, eat at night"
he said, and was joyful
nobody told him he was suffering
from Bulimia
he thought he was healthy;
after a matchless life,
he died clapping and singing

I GOTTA TAKE CARE OF MICHEL
Café Montmartre, Copenhagen 1986

"He stepped down, he cracked his leg,
he hasn't walked this whole tour.
Every time, I say it's the last — I have girlfriends.
I met this flute player in Amsterdam —
it's tough, you can't get back at the guy,
so you have to tease him, like brothers —
now he's fucked up his leg
and I have to carry him —
he left his crutches on the train —
he has no crutches.
He fired Marianne before he left,
felt she wasn't creative enough for his career —
he sent her a note, he didn't tell me —
now he's got Gessman, I don't know him,
he's going to last two weeks, he was creating problems
I dunno
Michel makes some funny bum decisions.
Maybe the guy will be good.
He says, Michel, I'm a sideman,
you don't give a shit about them —
Michel wants to leave a day early to see his —
he may be on a star trip now
I dunno
a manager like that, so pretentious —
Michel says next year he wants First Class,
he's going through a lot of things with his personal life,
his old lady —
if you wanna be single be single, you know
but you can't
— Genghis Khan, you know — in Rome,
I get to the club, crash, man, crash,
I was carrying Michel —
that night he was drunk, E. comes up,
well you just adjust to this: I said
I gotta take care of Michel"

CONSIDER YOUR ENEMIES

Consider your enemies and forgive them
you will know them by their numinosity.
Brains and blood running on a wall in Beirut
is of a more fearful colour
than the same stuff in a pub in Ireland
where at least they speak English.
And the child molester in Stanley Park
has edges, and the body of the child
has edges, and her terrible death was a death.
Consider how the peoples of Eastern Europe
crouching by television sets in Rumania for instance
                                        or Poland
reacted as the events of the State of Emergency
reached them from Quebec, consider
the Palestinian child with his stone,
consider his counterpart in South Africa,
if a boy were crushed
by a gang's car here in Vancouver
you would not be half so afraid.
And when the bomb bursts in Cyprus or the Sikh
temple flowers in fire in Pakistan
there are no edges, there is no end to it.
"Beirut," says a Lebanese friend, "was like Paris
of the Republic, and now,
it is almost as bad as Belfast."

They are striking again in Poland,
the picture trembles when we try to see it,
even when they speak, and are telling us
"It is not as bad as you thought.
We were not so good, or the others
more evil than in your own country.
We were concerned with bread, houses,
money, and the right to choose.
We died simply, every death,
taken on its own, was simple,
on this street, if we were lucky, by this known wall,
and held by a friend."

35

FROM THE INTERIOR

Dear Jim I have lost some will or
needful serious intent
nothing advances
in the world's work or mine
elsewhere the killing continues
made marginal by clutter
my human personal junk
the wrong place for the right reasons —
this is inexcusable.
I can't judge distances,
I am travelling neither towards you
nor away from you
I wish something were required of me
difficult and absolute
and I knew what it was.

Today I am crossing the prairies,
your kind of landscape — peripheral,
the fields ochre and green,
the sky toneless cerulean,
monitored by small clouds
of variable whites, while under them
we enter areas of darkness
without a lurch or sound —
the way the mind by stealth
enters the ordinary habit of despair.
How can such insubstantials
cast such density? as if the earth
were torn apart
and some kind of burnt, subcutaneous
surface exposed but the edge
as we enter is not torn,
it is smooth and silent.

The shadow dilates with the eye,
the details of the fields are indelible amber.
We have to love what we have.
We go on,
we graze with our mouths pressed against the earth,
till it can't bear us any longer.

EXECUTION OF PIMPS AND PROSTITUTES
Busher, Iran, April 1989

Scenario: a stadium — and perhaps
(they do not write this)
daylight, an almost shadowless burning sun.
I am not, for once, one of the lookers-on,
I smell their gusto distantly, their hush
of thirst and apprehension.
I am what they came
to be delivered from.

One trench? or many, measured holes? The human
form, in life, is mostly narrow and upright,
as we are now.
Loose piles of earth beside us, shovels and stones.

We are, after all, eleven — and the four men.
They're covered only to the waist.
Are their arms bound, are they
hooded or naked? (here I withdraw,
I do not know about
the details, the truth
is one of these, the mind's light,
mercifully indifferent, touches them equally).
There is a continuous ritual shout,
or there is silence, absolute.
The Shia judge has decreed "small stones"
so that death will be slow.

We are standing deeper now.
Oh my companions, hapless and impure,
history's rubbish, as we ever were.
And is this not a kind of tenderness,
that they have covered up our breasts?
How good they are!
How their eyes blaze with shame and fire!

INSTANTLY IT WAS A WORD
for Ahmad

Where I was looping and sewing
and pulling the thread
tight, what emerged
was a word. And you saw it.
You took the pen out of my hand
and the same lines
slid off, but swift, ardent and accurate.

I am writing in the heavy soluble
liquid of mirrors,
my mind's looped back
into its own reflection, I recognize
nothing, if you say these are words
I have to take your word for it,
I am the last one
of generations this prank was played upon,
on dirt, on slate, on paper — the word
paper that wrote itself whitely,
and appeared. I am stepping backwards
awkward into a secret avenue and my shadow
repeats each difficult glyph, slow icon and rune.
A word, and one more step —
and space for it in the sand.

MY TOM WAYMAN
(in answer to his "My Neruda" article in Event)

Dear Tom
would it have killed you to learn Spanish?
Maybe I've always wondered why your poems
sound like good translations of your poems.
And how can you rely
on Bly?
Here I am up to the wrists in terrible Arabic
all because of a man called Darwish
who writes like nobody else alive
and there was Neruda's pure music and the absolute
choice of a word
lying flat across the opposing page of your book
as useless as if you were blind and deaf
and you never insisted?

There is a greed in me
that shakes at the stem of my brain
like a terrier, it has teeth
and appetite and won't rest
I must eat these poems and drink them
word for word, it will take years,
they drive against me like leaves in wind, like ash;
and Darwish is not dead, he is still writing,
even as I strive at the almost inedible
        roots of his passionate grammar,
somewhere in Paris
he has quietly pulled a piece of
        paper towards him, he is writing another poem.

LEARNING ARABIC
The eye of the needle of passion is very narrow - Rumi

It is a needle's eye
into that country,
most difficult
narrowed to expectancy
to being foolish, mute,
naked, without the cloth of names.

I am erased.
What is the word for eye,
this plunge sears the cortex
scorched clean
I am moving into regions
of violence and delicacy
they are consumed with meaning
they are empty.

Something is lifting over the desert
I am to / wards it
precognitive
I am the face facing it
my mouth opens,
God's mouth, solving.

The thread is a human hair
it emerges substanceless
its cells
reassemble
it begins to write
it crosses the page, its dimensions
subsume, it becomes
a curve of inarticulate absence.
It cuts, repeatedly.
Something impales itself,
a cipher, a pattern of particles.

The clear stream
light
I am walking without
the word for feet,
across that light
what is it, wading upwards?
Its sleeves breathe,
Its breast is a forehead
there is a sound
there is a word for the sound of light
no one has discovered it.
My inner arms and
the water's light, there,
something, some feel,
there is a space between
the surface and the light
my face is dissolving
at its peripheries
there are motes
counted on the fingers of motes.

When I lost the word for forest
a space opened.

I am enraptured by these silences,
azures, infinites.
They extend, they interpret the face of my face
they exist here, here the light finds them,
there is no contamination.

Lean down, in the crevasse
between two names is the being
between red and azure
water and its skin
the moon's limb and the moon
the cut and the act
the fall and the impact
my face and its facing.

The word deflects
falls to the side by grace
it is the iron toothcap
over the evident flower,
it is the camera
transfixing the wing's beat
it is familiar
it has a finish.

Wait
in the interstices
the new names wait for their naming
pressed to my forehead like water
    on the twin fingers of God:
Alef, Beh, Teh

SUDDENLY I SAW YOU ON TV

There you were. The swarmed screen
opening in the centre of the crowd: Jerusalem
a parade for the Resurrection — and this priest
his white sleeves fallen back from his raised arms
holding two torches, and striding on
while people pressed at the procession
to light their fires from his.
He was you — your burly beard, your stare —
he walked without faltering though they pressed
he did not stoop, they had to accommodate
him and his purpose — he had a grim look, absolute.

A narrow life, you'd say, this man with your face
and a whole year's tiresome ritual between each flaring
and dangerous Easter over the washed stones.
You make do with less passionate magic,
rejecting not too tantalizing gifts
at best you'll end up with a rapt shore
and the tide running in and still no words
you'd find acceptable.
There he goes, with no quarrel.
Only an image, wrenched to sight and lost.
Quick, as he thrusts in your face his face
and holds out one twin fire
with his wrist's ardent complicity.

THE REFUGEE CENTRE, COPENHAGEN

made a facade for visitors and hung
garlands and masks by children, artwork on a wall
hurried into white. Down the dirty hall
your room might be the hidden real
or a change of scene — *Act Two: Dusk* —
the old smell, and silence
without bright Danish interference.
And I know now why it frightens me —
the bunks — outsize, towering
right and left — a child's scared eye
sees them, the same eye
that stared at photos of the Liberation.
No faces peer white and uncanny
with that starved subcuticular grin.
We sit on low chairs, with our backs turned.
You were not born then.
You speak all evening of Gaza.

GERMANY IN MID-DISTANCE

Only the great stations, and the cold rooms
of houses in Uelzen where I drew
on canvas the rich — their silks, pearls,
even a monocle, and a gaitered wooden leg.
They had threatening dogs, I remember now,
and several kinds of *wurst* in the mornings.
Wo waren Sie im Jahren '41?
One in a U-boat, survived to strut
in his seventies and preen
(his upright stance, his wavy hair)
before the mirrors at Bad Bevensen.
One drove me in Lübecker Heide
and failed to mention Belsen through the trees.

And now you, Jameel, gone to Berlin, fed up
with Denmark, letting your life
turn where it will, fragile plans
in your hand, memories
not mine, your shaken years
'48 though you were not born
and '82 when death
left you for dead —
I am deluded as always, to think I am safe,
to think I will see you again,
to think it matters.

KASTRUP, NOVEMBER AFTERNOON

After a bad summer, the early dark
astonishes, at three
the arrival hall's gloomy and flagless. The door puffs
like a faint cheer, and passengers from Malmø
emerge and no one meets them.
The screen rolls. From Japan
something's approaching, steady and dead on time.
Your plane's so late (*Damask-Berlin*)
it's not even "estimated". After an hour I ask.
To wait it out, or leave —
you're neither child nor lover. Hunched in the bus
back to the city, I think of you
stuck in the airport at Berlin,
or in the grounded plane,
or in the stormy sky over Europe,
cruel, thoughtless history smoking past the windows —
outside the bus, lights and their reflections
slide off, deadened by the heavier dark.

HIND, EATING FISH IN DENMARK

Hind with her long red nail
peels out the eye of the herring
(smoked the colour of lead or leather
flattened like the bog bodies
found under fake hills
in this northern land of her exile)

peels it out, eats it
while I protest and say
something vague about
poisonous concentrations of Vitamin A
imagining (behind the print
of articles that I forget)
more north, Greenland, the gutted seal
or yellowish bear dead on the snow
the polar liver, the extreme eye —

then I remember the island, the dogs' plate,
where I dumped codfish cooked with rye
bread, and, inside the courtyard
halfdoor, safe from their marauding,
whole fish-heads for the cats, cooling on yesterday's
news.

Later, going in with a broom,
I'd sweep up jaws more brittle than a bird's,
tiny concave saucers that had held a cheek of meat,
crescents of gills, and knitting needle bones
chewed clean even of their smell,
deserted by the flies.

But, there would be an eye — !
skidding under the broom-edge, berry white,
another one — no nick, no pupil, nothing to hold it by.
The dogs, too, nosed them high and dry
in their slicked dish. Animals know,
just like the Esquimaux.

Hind, daintily eating between white teeth,
laughs at me. Her Iraqi name
means India. Don't, Hind, it will grow
out of your forehead, first a sear
small as the end of a cigarette, then a swollen scar
long and almond, with lashes painted on.
It will wink at us and stare.

REFUGEE SWIMMING, FREDERIKSBERG BATHS

How easily, dangerously one condescends!
The teacher is a nice, trim Dane,
cropped hair, flat belly, strides
on the tiles, orders us almost apologetically and smiles,
the smallest of signals.
Only we, in the water,
pick it up like seals
with our unerring animal radar.
The big one from Somalia,
her firm black flesh bulging
in the sleeved gymsuit, and the pregnant
Iranian with her long hair
streaming on the surface and
(seen in the showers)
the beard
in the small of her back,
combed vertical by the water,
and me, not eligible,
foreign enough to try,
and lovely Hind, gasping.

We tread water with a vengeance,
our eyes fixed on our teacher
as students ought
but a touch meeker, a touch
(because we have learned) compliant,
responding to that flicker of a sign,
that tiny *übermensch*
behind her eyes.

Once there was a word
(we are splashing and trying)
— *paternalist* — the Danes
treated "their" Inuit so —
it's not racism oh no it's not
you need
to be down here in the water to notice it
down here kicking to the count
remembering to breathe
while the walls
gleam and echo to her voice
her niceness, the fact that she'd deny
any of this, and I
too, back in my clothes and
cycling down Gotersgade
my blue eyes
adequate disguise
that glance at dark families shopping on the street
and before I can kill it
change, just
imperceptibly

LEARNING TO SWIM

at this late date, even,
reminds me of learning to fly
which never actually happened
the top of 34th where the roads
went downhill in both directions, Blenheim Street
with its soft edges I used to pretend
were country lanes in the Lake District
little romantic
Mother reading Wordsworth in the afternoons

Flying however was secret, the day
chosen by some now lost numerology
something to do with the first spring day
you went to school with only a cardigan
wool buttons, you loved their nipple and colour
and being all by yourself at the exact time
and your feet even in oxfords pushing off
upward — it would be so easy
if it had worked

I don't remember
my disappointment, only my faith
Learning to swim really, at fifty six
surprised at my surprise more than anything,
at how difficult turns into easy

The refugees sink like sacks at the shallow end
laughing and struggling
while I
strike out for Sweden
or somewhere, my head that I've been pushing
a/head of me all this time like a grim ball
water logged so it won't float
nestles in, floats perfectly
a prow, peerless, the transparent
turquoise butting and parting —
no neck stalk straining
I've stopped having a neck and parts

I'm one of those fish
with the funny eyes half over and half under
chlorine washes through me like laughter
I am green, I am inside out,
I see the earth like astronauts, my noisy globe
rolls me — how would you feel
if this was it, I mean maybe dying
isn't so bad, though naturally
you'd have to learn as you were drowning.

SWIMMING LANES

are like shipping lanes
Suez Canal
the drab little crossing
the truck labeled *Tourist's Police*
with gunsight holes in the canvas
that preceded us from the border out of Gaza
rafted over with one bus (Masada Tours)
and thirteen passengers
a dog makes the trip as well
why not, says his look
bored soldiers
watch from the low bank
there are two men fishing
and behind us on the hills
the burnt-out tanks
of a different war

while bearing down on us
there's no other term for it
full term, huger than anything else in sight
ship after ship from the south
with no room to spare
freighters, container platforms
steep sides pressed past
24 hours towards the Mediterranean
longest green light in the world
then 24 hours the other way
spice routes, silk roads
passage to India (of course you know
the origin of the word Posh)
oil licks at the sand's edge
and Suez crossing
no more than a post,
a little gray road that dips and resumes,
and the ferry getting itself over
in the calm
between monster ships

After Ismailia
at a shop, hardly a village
we wait with our escort
while the bustling little Pakistani salesman
maybe just to shame the Egyptians
runs in with his rug to pray

Swimming lanes, then,
have their own unwritten signals and regulations
the pool's not roped off and you look
cautiously for the least traffic
you strike out where it seems clear
how do you know though
if that man in the goggles
whose head is bobbing forward towards you
hasn't been swimming here for twenty seasons
are you crowding him? how do you know
he won't change lanes suddenly
even now in passing, his foot
lashing out
grazes your shoulder
you see underwater
his lapping belly
the little blobs in his trunks

you would rather have
Suez, it seems, your own inviolable lane
secured by narrowing sand on both sides,
no oncoming threats, and the tiny ferry
irrelevant under your bows.

STONED TO DEATH IN THE NETHER LANDS

They were seldom stoned to death in the Nether Lands,
there are no stones,
deltas of silt and salt estuaries
fires seen at a distance along the dikes
great skies etherizing human ash
and the blood of Passchendaele and Aachen
spread in the level water where famine
long before Dürer's turf or Rembrandt's trees
among the grass stalks and bent stems
foundered up to the knees.

Whereas here it seldom rains
but the land's rich with them, they lie
everywhere and have lain
in their silence shaking in the heat, the earth
yields them over and over
out of fields surfacing,
little flowers without penitence, more than enough.
They fell outward of Jericho, their echo
shudders in the vales, and from the razed town
raked free of thorns, they are shimmering,
and from this morning's rubble
domestic and ancient with promise.

And if there is no rain
to scrape them clean there is time
time for each small
hand unborn or groping at a breast,
for each hand the shape of a stone,
for each stone a skull.

THE CHAPEL OF THE ASCENSION

The boys wheel the souvenir cart in and lock the door —
it is sundown. Away beyond and below,
the Dead Sea in its trough sucks the last light under
and Jordan melts in improbable pink and azure.
I looked in earlier — at the gate
a boy demanded a shekel, then followed me in.
There is a sunk stone, lined like a bath,
the place is otherwise empty.
The dome's bald interior
the same rough stone, and no chair or altar.
The boy recited that the dent in the rock
is Christ's print
when He took off. Harder for Him now,
with a low door and only four small windows
glazed and screened. But a sparrow darts, lands
on a glass edge where it's broken, and slips through —
anything's possible —

And now all night the souvenirs
inhabit the Chapel of the Ascension
toy camels carved in olive wood
leave their place and nod across the post cards,
rosaries tell themselves in whispers,
the maps flare and subside.

SOME POEMS 'RELATED TO THE DRAWINGS'

There are no poems.
There is the work
but no words for it, to write poems
would be like making paintings afterwards,
deliberate and contaminated.
I could write down
what I did not draw —
a way of telling it, maybe, simply,
with no conclusions.

1

What I did not draw in the West Bank

The house in the valley under the bare hills
the single room the open door
the orange trees close around it
dark waxy green light, fruit like lanterns,
the fire in the brazier, the good food, the laughter,
the red-cheeked girl, Ghada, dancing,
the laughter
gunfire from the camp
two little boys running across a field

2

What I did not draw in Khan Younis

Imaan in the early morning
in silence, in a white nightdress
and bare feet, dressing her little sisters
stepping over the inert form of her brother
bypassing her snoring grandmother
rolling up mats, folding the blankets,
as in a slow dance, evenly,
Imaan at sixteen with her hair knotted
sweeping out the house, the dark red gorgeous rugs
with a short, stiff broom, stooping,
the door open, the spring light entering
from the terrace, the row of shoes,
the chill light entering,
Imaan straightening to glance out across the camp,
Imaan who will never be this beautiful again —
when she passes I touch her white foot with my hand
it is ice cold

3

What I did not draw in Jerusalem

The interior of the Red Crescent ambulance
as we descend from the Mount of Olives
into Jerusalem, dust, sunlight outside, the unsmiling boy
propped on the bench between us, his useless legs
dangling, going home to Gaza,
Akram on the floor, the tube taped to his face
his arms clenched his eyes staring —
at Damascus Gate tanks, mounted border guards,
stink of tear gas and the crowd running.
We pull the blinds we go slow
then fast / out of Jerusalem lurching on bad springs
Akram's brother leans down at every curve
and steadies his head
with a large hand, patiently, then pours
a measure of juice into the tube
and, pulling a crumpled paper out of his pocket,
unfolds it, carefully writes the amount on it.

It isn't that I did not grieve:
people ask me, what did I feel,
or whether, while I stood there drawing,
I would have refused comfort.
I don't know —
there were so many comforters.
One night Suhaib, for once without
mother, father, nurse
nearly rolled out of bed
and I put down my things and lifted him in again.
I don't know if that counts.
It wasn't comfort.

I remember Dr. Dajani
who was certainly compassionate,
passionate even, running to me with an extracted bullet
and how heavy it felt pressed into my palm.
It had just been lifted
out of a child's forehead.
But then, if he was weeping,
he wasn't actually operating.
Tears blur the work, for me
the ache is a line, accurate as I can make it.
I can't cry just then
because I have to pay attention to a child.

THE RUSSIAN COMPOUND
for Leah Tsemel

From that place
I came to inadvertently
under Jerusalem
not cool, the air
much breathed, thick,
I thought it was a courtroom
I'd lost my way
and the slouched guards
would let me through if I asked.

Draw me, one said when I tried
to bargain with him
I remember his head
muscular, pouting and proud
even now I could tell it
feature by feature
to an artist or a computer
not to myself, though I thirst
after it as if I were in love
and then bereaved.
Those are the cells, he said, and grinned.
Draw me. But he would not let me through
and I was careless then, I refused.

I found the room upstairs, the boys
you'd told me of,
three "children of the stones" —
they staggered, chained at the feet,
in a row, handcuffed,
parody of the *dabkah,* the dance,
and that same guard
had to dance as well
as he brought them in, with his wrist
locked to the wrist of the first.

HUMAN ACTS

Twelve men and boys
taken in a raid
driven to an olive grove away from the village
the orders were to break their arms and legs.
Soldiers who didn't want to do it
could go and sit in the jeep.
As for the last man,
they broke only his arms.
That was / so he could walk back
and tell what happened.

Was it nearly dawn when he got there?
These paths, the twisted road are known to him
like his own hands, like the faces of his children.
He cradles the split arm
with the one he still can move
high against his chest, it has become
outside himself, he could be carrying a lamb
or a child. He whispers.
There is enough light, anyway,
and over this ridge
the village in terrible silence.

FOR THE SOLDIERS

Any one of you
could have been my son
your forgivable
glowing skin / I'm proud of
your roving eye
your bear's strength
loose of my old knots
walking out in the world where it's
white and dangerous

I'm off Mom what I do
hasn't to do with you

I'll draw you then
empty as I know how
no regrets, no late advice
(my eye won't tell
what my hand has seen)

slouched by a wall, or on the run
and staring upwards, with all
the obscene paraphernalia —

and what you write
in those abrupt, square
letters building stone by stone
Masada and Jerusalem
I won't read

any more than I can read your eyes
secret and arrogant and no more mine
than Simon, Daniel, Benjamin

THE POEM WALKED OUT

The poem walked out and it did not
know where to put itself
it entered the eye of a young soldier
and was extinguished.
The boot of a soldier crushed it in the road
several shadows of running children crossed it
it began to speak,
in the noise of gunfire it was interrupted
and changed into little pieces of sound.
A girl lifted it between her fingers
but it withered. The light fell on it
and was blinded. The poem wrote itself
across the back of a man walking
into the hills near Tayasir
no one explained it. All day it clung
between his shoulders, it attempted to comfort him
the poem was not adequate.
It began to be ashamed.
The man took it off and folded it carefully
and put it down.
He sat on a stone beside the poem
with one hand on his knee and one hand
covering the poem. It became dark.

FACING NORTH

It was like entering an alien country,
this homecoming. First
Cyprus in sunlight under the El Al plane,
then clouded Europe and the dark,
waking up to absence morning after morning,
apprehension after the event —

that walk through *Kongens Have* on an early Sunday
after a night of poetry and intemperate plans,
your face, Ahmad, when you saw across the grass
four isolated men, each one alone with a child
irresolute by the water, or at the desolate swings:
"Who are they?" "Oh," I said, "the weekend fathers."
and your look, as if you had been struck.

What is this grief, this region? Denmark, where I drew
with my class all day at the *sportshal* in Lyngby,
"The Figure in Motion" and I chose
pool players, solid concentrated men
drawing them over and over as they leaned flat out
across the tables, repeating the same move
(elbow raised, sighting along the cue)
and I thought, this is peace then, a full stomach,
orderly play, the same week after week,
and taking it for granted.

I cannot, I have become foreign,
out of heat and peril I find myself unable
to return to normal, I am facing north
it seems all wrong to be here, to be lonely,
to be at peace, I am staring
as if from that barbed place
where the sun
is vertical and intimate, where the act
signifies, and no one
is abandoned, and nothing is certain.

ON BEING HATED

The first was a Jewish boy at Queen's, clean shaven,
mostly silent, his silence was like
the kind you hear on the cancer wards,
white, painful. When he spoke
the words were like nails, hurting him,
but he did not wince. His body was rigid.
Was his heart pounding? Mine was.
How his gentle classmates blurred, how he grew,
branched, metastasized!
I made this happen, I caused this ill
of will, this private violation.
I am sorry, I want to put my hands
on his face but he can't see me
I am here at the podium, he is seated over to the right,
between us is absolute negative space,
stretched skin to skin, and no help for it.

ALL YOU HAVE DONE

Hind spoke for me on the phone.
"It was a man's voice, not Nawaal's.
He said almost nothing.
Almost, he did not
acknowledge the greeting....
After all you have done."
I am silenced. The phone, at least,
relented after days of static.
Who is listening in? Where
(I want to believe)
were the letters intercepted?
At times one envelope
appears, simply,
an unlikely flimsy blue,
the address upended with *Danemark* first,
as I write *Gaza, via Israel.*
This is not personal.

The camp's dust lifts
and interferes, words are inadequate,
to be there face to face is inadequate.
"I am trying to learn the language."
I would go now,
if my hand did not have to drag
my whole body with it, disappointed in love and
hungry for small returns.
My whole body and all it has done.

While downstairs the landlord
scowls when he hears the voices
is there if he can make it (down two flights)
to close the street door
in the face of my guests.

Copenhagen, August 1990

RØDBY-PUTTGARTEN CROSSING
August 25, 1990

Presumably even a small
jellyfish is thoughtful, is happy,
floating in the calm water,
greenly, under the surface,
warm in August.
The wake pulls them softly, and rolls them
they bell and extend
they are almost passive
they extend to their boundaries
and are content
conscious
of light and its directions,
of their centres,
and their extension to their boundaries.
They lift in the wake,
candles, smocked muslin
muscle in two dimensions,
pink parody of lungs,
thought-bubbles from the comics,
solar discs — floppy ones,
storing, out of all we have in common
what seems moral and good to them

The huge prow of the ferry
is stubby, it does not slice them
they are far from the grit of beaches
and Puttgarten there low on the horizon
they drift in their hundreds
unurgent, blameless, baffled
by a wavery line of weed and ruck

When war was declared, Mother told,
"It was the most beautiful, late summer day,
at the end of summer, 1939 — "

And now
this light,
calm dermis of the water,
stretched, puckered like a zwieback
clouded with submergent, happy thought —
it is my skin I am crossing
this is my ignorant body
these are my happy cells

NEWS OF WAR

The phone, and we're out of sleep
one of the young men
saying irreparable things.
How did I get into this?
You fling yourself against my arms
as if I were a coat
you fling off. Floor, walls, furniture
are as much use. Your face
pulled into its exaggerations, hideous.
Shit, you say in your infallible woman's voice,
Shit Denmark, shit Bush, shit the people.
You run from room to room, switching on lights.
I'm trying to get the BBC and you're screaming.

MAP 1

Taleb has xeroxed a map of Baghdad,
he brought it today and left,
about A3, the lines grayish,
there on the kitchen table
Hind's hands on it, her face
bent over it, she is not here,
not crying right now, her finger moves and touches:
Look, this is Palestina Street, here
we lived, this is our house, at this corner.
All that was hit, all that area.
And this is the power plant, all that area
finished, burning. Her voice is almost inaudible.
She is silent, staring,
the weight of her hands gentle,
her finger unfists, traces the looping river.
See, she begins again,
how the river turns, it is beautiful really,
see how beautiful it is
she is silent
the map, under her hands
before I can prevent this,
bandages, death, a death.

MAP 2

No high-tech laser
sees what she sees
no penile missile with a camera in its finger
telling, like the *Book of the Dead*
what it was like to die,
her eyes
inches from the page
feeling towards impact
taking out
with more precision
than any gun's mad funeral video
Palestina Street, there
where the lines cross, innocent
house, sills the colour of honey,
bedding on the roof unrolled at dusk,
tactile innumerable detail
childhood's indelible voices and faces
scent of
mother, bread, lemon

MOTHER OF BATTLES 1

Today I come in and
Hind's managed to get
Om Al-Ma'rik on short wave at 21.9
Mother of Battles Radio fills the flat
happy soldiers who entered a Saudi town
interviewed and the music I guess
equivalent to military marches in America
encouraging heroics —
Hind translates, her voice not saddened,
"The enemy ran away, they could not defeat us."

CNN says they are "encircled",
a nice word, like "surgical"
yesterday they showed, once,
a sudden flagrant rage of the earth,
called it "the impact of an
Area Denial Weapon" —
but showing it was a mistake
and will not be repeated
cluster bombs
not fit for video vocabulary

Hind's only brother Ali
is somewhere in Kuwait he had no choice
perhaps in one of the "armored personnel carriers"
7 were "taken out surgically"
if still alive he eats once a day
he is according to General Schwartzkopf
infested with lice
he says "They could not defeat us" on
Mother of Battles Radio

Hind do not be
glad how can I say this
be what you must I am not a creepy
crisis psychologist listing
the clinical stages of your despair
I will hear
from now on Mother of Battles Radio
why not get all the lies and stories
possible, so we can choose,
secretly, whatever will comfort us —
from minute to minute and day to day,
like milk or the touch of a hand.

MOTHER OF BATTLES 2

"They have said,
some of the Moroccans
are refusing to fight their brothers,
and then the Americans
started to shoot them — "
Mother of Battles Radio news
and I'm half way out the door
I have to bring myself
to lift my eyes, after all
you came after me to tell me

poster look
straight, bright I have seen your
slap-up slogan face
in Chinese calendars
Cuban or Nicaraguan magazines
El Salvador SWAPO how dead flat
and clean and defiant
your large round eyes your gaze
that hate has made innocent

Something tastes bad on the stairs
someone was sick, maybe
or, it's the enzyme factory
on Hillerød Street
and the wind's the wrong way

Other Wolsak and Wynn books
by Heather Spears:

How to Read Faces, 1986
 (Pat Lowther Award)

The Word for Sand, 1988
 (Pat Lowther Award, and
 Governor General's Award for Poetry)